SELF-DEVELOPMENT AND THE WAY TO POWER

L. W. Rogers

HAWK PRESS

Published by

Hawk Press
4836/24, Ansari Road, Daryaganj
New Delhi – 110 002
Phones: +91-11-23278618, +91-11-43667199
E-mail: thehawkpress@gmail.com
www.thehawkpress.com

"We may be either the suffering slaves of nature or the happy masters of her laws."

SELF DEVELOPMENT AND
THE WAY TO POWER

It is the natural right of every human being to be happy—to escape all the miseries of life. Happiness is the normal condition, as natural as the landscapes and the seasons. It is unnatural to suffer and it is only because of our ignorance that we do suffer. Happiness is the product of wisdom. To attain perfect wisdom, to comprehend fully the purpose of life, to realize completely the relationship of human beings to each other, is to put an end to all suffering, to escape every ill and evil that afflicts us. Perfect wisdom is unshadowed joy.

Why do we suffer in life? Because in the scheme of nature we are being forced forward in evolution and we lack the spiritual illumination that alone can light the way and enable us to move safely among the obstacles that lie before us. Usually we do not even see or suspect the presence of trouble until it suddenly leaps upon us like a concealed tiger. One day our family circle is complete and happy. A week later death has come and gone and joy is replaced with agony. Today we have a friend. Tomorrow he will be an enemy and we do not know why. A little while ago we had wealth and all material luxuries. There was a sudden change and now we have only poverty and misery and yet we seek in vain for a reason why this should be.

There was a time when we had health and strength; but they have both departed and no trace of a reason appears. Aside from these greater tragedies of life innumerable things of lesser consequence continually bring to us little miseries and minor heartaches. We most earnestly desire to avoid them but we never see them until they strike us, until in the darkness of our ignorance we blunder upon them.

The thing we lack is the spiritual illumination that will enable us to look far and wide, finding the hidden causes of human suffering and revealing the method by which they may be avoided; and if we can but reach illumination the evolutionary journey can be made both comfortably and swiftly. It is as though we must pass through a long, dark room filled with furniture promiscuously scattered about. In the darkness our progress would be slow and painful and our bruises many. But if we could press a button that would turn on the electric light we could then make the same journey quickly and with perfect safety and comfort.

The old method of education was to store the mind with as many facts, or supposed facts, as could be accumulated and to give a certain exterior polish to the personality. The theory was that when a man was born he was a completed human being and that all that could be done for him was to load him up with information that would be used with more or less skill, according to the native ability he happened to be born with.

The theosophical idea is that the physical man, and all that constitutes his life in the physical world, is but a very partial expression of the self; that in the ego of each there is practically unlimited power and wisdom; that these may be brought through into expression in the physical world as the physical body and its invisible counterparts, which together constitute the complex vehicle of the ego's manifestation, are evolved and adapted to the purpose; and that in exact proportion that conscious effort is given to such self-development will spiritual illumination be achieved and wisdom attained. Thus the light that leads to happiness is kindled from within and the evolutionary journey that all are making may be robbed of its suffering.

Why does death bring misery? Chiefly because it separates us from those we love. But when we have evolved the faculty of clairvoyance, in our work of self-development, the separation vanishes and our "dead" friends are as much with us as the living. The only other reason why death brings grief or fear is because we do not understand it and comprehend the part it plays in human evolution. But the moment our ignorance gives way to comprehension such fear vanishes and a serene happiness takes its place.

Why do we have enemies from whose words or acts we suffer? Because in our limited physical consciousness we do not perceive the unity of all life and realize that our wrong thinking and doing must react upon us through other people—a situation from which there is no possible escape except through ceasing to think evil and then patiently awaiting the time when the causes we have already generated are fully exhausted. When spiritual illumination comes, and we no longer stumble in the night of ignorance, the last enemy will disappear and we shall make no more forever.

Why do people suffer from poverty and disease? Only because of our blundering ignorance that makes their existence possible for us, and because we do not comprehend their meaning and their lessons, nor know the attitude to assume toward them. Had we but the wisdom to understand why they come to people, why they are necessary factors in their evolution, they would trouble us no longer. When nature's lesson is fully learned these mute teachers will vanish.

And so it is with all forms of suffering we experience. They are at once reactions from our ignorant blunderings and instructors that point out the better way. When we have comprehended the lessons they teach they are no longer necessary and disappear.

Thus our evolution is going forward and has gone forward in the past. We know that the human race has passed through a long evolution during which it has acquired five senses by which knowledge is gained. Nobody who has given thought to the subject will make the mistake of supposing that this evolution is completed and that the five senses are all we shall ever possess.

In this long evolutionary journey the next thing we shall do is to develop the sixth sense. Some people have already done so and all are approaching it. This dawning sense is called clairvoyance. Fair investigation will show that the clairvoyant possesses certain powers not common to the majority of people.

This is merely the beginning of the development of the sixth sense, and probably with the majority of clairvoyants it goes no further than etheric and lower astral sight. In other words, they are able to raise the consciousness only to a grade of matter a little beyond the grasp of ordinary vision, while the properly developed, trained clairvoyant raises his consciousness two full planes beyond.

The higher the consciousness is raised the further the horizon of knowledge extends and the clairvoyant is able to hand down information that appears quite miraculous; but it is perfectly natural. If a certain person were born blind and had never understood any more about eyesight than most people understand about clairvoyance; if this person could know how many doorways were in a large building only by groping along with his hands and thus acquiring the knowledge by touch, and another person who could see should glance along the block and instantly tell the blind man the correct number, that would be to the blind man a miracle.

Now, when a clairvoyant sees things at a distance where the physical eye cannot reach he really does nothing more remarkable. When we see a thing we receive the vibrations caused by light. That gives the information. When the clairvoyant "sees" at a distance through what we mistakenly call solid substances he receives vibrations of matter so fine that it interpenetrates solids as the ether does.

Every human being must make, and is making, this long evolutionary journey from spiritual infancy to godlike power and perfection, but there are two ways in which it may be done. We may, as the vast majority do, accept the process of unconscious evolution and submit to nature's whip and spur that continuously urge the thoughtless and indifferent forward until they finally reach the goal. Or, we may choose conscious evolution and work intelligently with nature, thus making progress that is comparatively of enormous rapidity and at the same time avoid much of what Hamlet called the "slings and arrows of outrageous fortune."

The degree to which mind can control circumstances and dominate matter is far greater than is generally believed. Our impressions about matter are very illusory. No form of matter is permanent. Change goes on everywhere at every instant, by physical laws in the physical body and by astral and mental laws in our invisible bodies.

We are not the same being, physically, mentally or spiritually, any two days in succession. The very soul itself is subject to this law of change. It may expand and shine out through the physical organism resplendent, or it may only faintly glimmer through a constantly coarsening body.

What is the law of soul growth? Through adherence to what principle may we reach spiritual illumination? There are certain well established facts about the laws of growth that we should not overlook when seeking the way forward. Nothing whatever can grow without use, without activity. Inaction causes atrophy. Physiologists tell us that if the arm be tied to the body so that it cannot be used it will in time become so enfeebled, that it is of no further service. It will wither away. That is nature's law of economy. She never gives life where it is useless, where it can not, or will not, be utilized.

On the other hand, exercise increases power. To increase the size and strength of muscles we must use them. This is just as true of mental and moral faculties as it is of the physical body. The only way to make the brain keen and powerful is to exercise it by original thinking.

One way to gain soul powers is to give free play to the loftiest aspirations of which we are capable, and to do it systematically instead of at random. We grow to be like the things we think about. Now, the reverse of all this must be equally true. To give no thought to higher things, to become completely absorbed in material affairs, is to stifle the soul, to invite spiritual atrophy.

Turning our attention to nature we shall find in the parasite convincing proof of all this. The parasite, whether plant or animal, is living evidence that to refuse or neglect to use an organ or faculty results in being deprived of it. The dodder, says Drummond, has roots like other plants, but when it fixes sucker discs on the branches of neighboring plants and begins to get its food through them, its roots perish. When it fails to use them it loses them. He also points to the hermit-crab as an illustration of this great fact in nature, that disuse means loss, and that to shirk responsibility is the road to degeneration.

The hermit-crab was once equipped with a hard shell and with as good means of locomotion as other crabs. But instead of courageously following the hardy life of other crustaceans it formed the bad habit of taking up its residence in the cast-off shells of mollusks.

This made life easy and indolent. But it paid the price of all shirking. In time it lost four legs, while the shell over the vital portion of its body degenerated to a thin membrane which leaves it practically helpless when it is out of its captured home. And this is the certain result of all shirking of responsibility. There may be an apparent temporary gain, but it always means greater loss, either immediate or remote. So nature punishes inaction with atrophy. Whatever is not used finally ceases to be. In plain language, apathy, inaction, idleness, uselessness, is the road to degeneration.

On the other hand, aspiration and activity mean growth, development, power.

So we grow, physically, mentally and morally, by activity, by exercise of the organs or the faculties we desire to possess. It is only by the constant exercise of these things that we can grow at all. When this great law of nature is understood we see at once how it is that life is full of trouble; why it is that the whole visible world seems to be designed to keep us constantly at work physically and mentally, to challenge our resourcefulness in improving our physical, social and political conditions, to continually try our patience and to forever test our courage. It is the way of development. It is the price of progress.

The universe is a training school for evolving intelligence—a vast gymnasium for the development of moral fibre. We become mentally clever by playing at the game of life. We match our courage against its adversities and acquire fearlessness. We try our optimism against its disappointments and learn cheerfulness. We pit our patience against its failures and gain persistence. We are torn from the pinnacle of ambition by opponents and learn toleration of others.

We fall from the heights of vanity and pride, and learn to be modest and humble. We encounter pain and sorrow and learn sympathy with suffering. It is only by such experiences that we can grow to rounded measure. It is only in an environment thus adapted to our spiritual development that we can evolve the latent powers within us.

Such is the universe in which we find ourselves and from it there is no escape. No man can avoid life—not even the foolish one who, when the difficulties before him appear for the moment overwhelming, tries to escape them by suicide. A man cannot die. He can only choose how he will live. He may either helplessly drift through the world suffering from all the ills and evils that make so many unhappy or he may choose the method of conscious evolution that alone makes life truly successful. We may be either the suffering slaves of nature or the happy masters of her laws.

Now, all powers possessed by any human being, no matter how exalted his position in evolution, or how sublime his spiritual power, are latent in all human beings and can, in time, be developed and brought into action.

Of course there is no magic rule by which the ignoramus can instantly become wise or by which a brutal man can be at once transformed into a saint. It may require scores of incarnations to accomplish a work so great, but when a man reaches the point in his evolution where he begins to comprehend the purpose of life, and to evolve the will to put forth his energies in co-operation with nature, his rise to wisdom and power may be swift indeed. But this transformation from the darkness of ignorance to spiritual illumination, from helplessness "in the fell clutch of circumstance" to power over nature, must be brought about by his own efforts, for it is a process of evolution—of forcing the latent to become the active. Therefore one must resolve to take oneself in hand for definite and systematic self-development. Nobody else can do the work for us.

Certain moral qualities must be gained before there can be spiritual illumination and genuine wisdom and such qualities, or virtues, have to be evolved by the laws under which all growth occurs. It is just as impossible to acquire a moral quality by reading about its desirability as to evolve muscular strength by watching the performance of a group of athletes. To gain muscular strength one must take part in the physical activities that produce it. He must live the athletic life. To win spiritual strength and supremacy he must live the spiritual life. There is no other way. He must first learn what mental and moral qualities are essential, and how to gain them, and then set earnestly about the work of acquiring them.

The first thing necessary is to get a clear understanding of the fact that the physical body is not the self but only a vehicle or instrument through which the self is being manifested in the visible world. The body is as much your instrument as the hand is, or as your pen is. It is a thing which you, the self, use and a clear conception of this fact—a feeling that this is the fact—is the first step toward that absolute control of the physical body that lays the foundation for success in conscious evolution. When we feel that in managing the physical body we are controlling something that is not ourself we are fairly started on the right road.

Now, there are three things that a person must possess to be successful in self-development. If he has not these three qualifications he will make but little progress; but, fortunately, any lacking quality can be evolved and if one does not possess these three necessities his first work is to create them. These three things are an ardent desire, an iron will and an alert intelligence. Why are these three qualifications essential to success and what purpose do they serve?

Desire is nature's motor power—the propulsive force that pushes everything forward in its evolution. It is desire that stimulates to action. Desire drives the animal into the activities that evolve its physical body and sharpen its intelligence. If it had no desire it would lie inert and perish. But the desire for food, for drink, for association with its kind, impel it to action, and the result is the evolution of strength, skill and intelligence in proportion to the intensity of its desires.

To gratify these desires it will accept battle no matter how great may be the odds against it and will unhesitatingly risk life itself in the combat. Desire not only induces the activity that develops physical strength and beauty, but also has its finer effects. Hunger compels the animal not only to seek food, but to pit its cunning against that of its prey. Driven forward by desire it develops, among other qualities, strength, courage, patience, endurance, intelligence.

Desire plays the same role with man at his higher stage of evolution. It stimulates him to action; and always as his activity satisfies his original desire a new one replaces the old and lures him on to renewed exertion.

The average young man beginning his business career, desires only a comfortable cottage. But when that is attained he wants a mansion. He soon tires of the mansion and wants a palace. Then he wants several—at the seaside, in the city, and on the mountains. At first he is satisfied with a horse; then he demands an automobile, and finally a steam yacht. He sets out as a youth to earn a livelihood and welcomes a small salary.

But the desire for money pushes him into business for himself and he works tirelessly for a competence. He feels that a small fortune should satisfy anybody but when he gets it he wants to be a millionaire. If he succeeds in that he then desires to become a multi-millionaire.

Whether the desire is for wealth, or for fame, or for power, the same result follows—when the desire is satisfied a greater one takes its place and spurs the ambitious one to still further exertion. He grasps the prize he believes to contain complete satisfaction only to discover that while he was pursuing it desire had grown beyond it, and so the goal he would attain is always far ahead of him.

Thus are we tricked and apparently mocked by nature until we finally awake to the fact that all the objects of desire—the fine raiment, the jewels, the palaces, the wealth, the power, are but vain and empty things; and that the real reward for all our efforts to secure them is not these objects at all but the new powers we have evolved in getting them; powers that we did not before possess and which we should not have evolved but for nature's great propulsive force—desire.

The man who accumulates a fortune by many years of persistent effort in organizing and developing a business enterprise, by careful planning and deep thinking, may naturally enough look upon the fortune he will possess for a few years before it passes on to others, as his reward. But the truth is that it is a very transient and perishable and worthless thing compared to the new powers that were unconsciously evolved in getting it—powers that will be retained by the man and be brought into use in future incarnations.

Desire, then, plays a most important role in human evolution. It awakens, stimulates, propels. What wind is to the ship, what steam is to the locomotive, desire is to the human being.

It has been written in a great book, "Kill out desire," and elsewhere it is written, "Resist not evil." We may find, in similar exalted pronouncements, truths that are very useful to disciples but which might be confusing and misleading to the man of the world if he attempted to literally apply them.

Perhaps for the average mortal "kill out desire" might be interpreted "transmute desire." Without desire man would be in a deathlike and dangerous condition—a condition in which further progress would be impossible. But by transmuting the lower desires into the higher he moves steadily forward and upward without losing the motive power that urges him forever onward.

To transmute desire, to continually replace the lower with the higher, really is killing desire out but it is doing it by the slow and safe evolutionary process. As to crushing it suddenly, that is simply impossible; but substitution may work wonders. Suppose, for example, that a young man is a gambler and his parents are much distressed about it.

The common and foolish course is to lecture him on the sin of gambling and to tearfully urge him to associate only with very proper young men. But the young gambler is not in the least interested in that sort of a life, which appears to him to be a kind of living death, and such entreaty does not move him.

His parents would do better by looking more closely into the case. Why is he a gambler? He desires money. He seeks excitement. He wants to live in an atmosphere of intense life and activity. Very well. These desires are quite right in themselves. It is useless to try to crush them. It is nonsense to argue that he does not want these things.

Clearly enough he does want them and that is precisely why he gambles. Then do not attempt the impossibility of killing the desire but change the objects of his desires. Say to him: "You desire money and a life full of turbulence and excitement. Well, you can get all that in a better and a legitimate way and have the respect of your friends besides. You can go into politics.

That is a field within the pale of the law and in it you can have scope for all the energy and activity and intensity of life you long for, with all the element of chance which you find so attractive." And when the young man has had his fling there and tires of it then something else can be attempted. But to try to crush desire and curb the outrushing life is both foolish and impossible. We can only direct it.

There are, of course, certain gross desires that must be gotten rid of by the most direct and least objectionable method, and when one really desires to be free from a given vice or moral weakness and sets earnestly and intelligently about it his release is not so difficult as the complete tyranny of most vices would lead one to suppose.

There is a process by which any of us may be free if we will take the trouble to patiently put it into practice. This method will apply to any desire from which we wish to be released. For example, let us take the person who has a settled desire for alcoholic stimulants but really wishes to be rid of it forever. Many people who are thus afflicted to the point where they occasionally become intoxicated feel, when they recover their normal condition, that no price would be too great to pay for freedom from this humiliating habit.

As a rule such a man tries to close his eyes to his shame and forget it, promising himself that he will be stronger when the temptation again assails him. But it is just this putting it aside, this casting it out of his mind, that perpetuates his weakness. He instinctively shrinks from dwelling upon the thought of whither he is drifting. So he puts the unpleasant subject aside altogether and when the inner desire asserts itself again he finds himself precisely as helpless as before.

Now, his certain method of escape from this tyranny of desire is to turn his mind resolutely to an examination of the whole question. Let him look the facts in the face, however humiliating they may be. He should call his imagination to his assistance. It should be used to picture to himself his future if he does not succeed in breaking up the unfortunate slavery of the desire nature. He should think of the fact that as he grows older the situation grows worse. He should picture himself as the helpless, repulsive sot, with feeble body and weakening mind, and reflect upon the humiliation he must endure, the poverty he must face, and the physical and mental pain he must bear in the future if he now fails to break the desire ties that bind him.

This creates in him a feeling of repulsion toward the cause of it all; and if he continues to think daily upon this hideous picture of what he is slowly drifting toward—if he daily regards it all with a feeling of slight repulsion—then even within a month or two he will find that his desire for drink is slowly fading out.

This is as true of all other desires that enslave us. The desire for alcoholic stimulants merely illustrates the principle involved. Any desire from which one wishes to be free may be escaped by the same method. But one who would free himself from the desire-nature should not make the mistake of creating a feeling of intense hostility toward the thing he seeks to escape; for hatred is also a tie. He should merely reach a position of complete indifference. He should think of it not with settled hostility, but with slight repulsion; and if he does that daily, mentally dwelling upon the pain and humiliation it causes, he will find the ties loosening, the desire weakening.

Desire is a force that may be beneficial or detrimental, according to its use. As we may eradicate a desire so may we create a desire. How, then, may one who seeks the highest self-development use desire, this propulsive force of nature, to help himself forward? He should desire spiritual progress most earnestly, for without such desire he cannot succeed. Therefore if the aspirant does not have the ardent desire for spiritual illumination he must create it.

To accomplish this let him again call imagination to his assistance. Let him picture himself as having his power for usefulness many times multiplied by occult development. He should think of himself as possessing the inner sight that enables him to understand the difficulties of others and to comprehend their sorrows. He should daily think of the fact that this would so broaden and quicken his sympathies that he would be enormously more useful in the world than he can now possibly be and that he could become a source of happiness to thousands.

Let him reflect that as he gets farther along in occult development and in unselfishness and spirituality he may have the inestimable privilege of coming into contact with some of the exalted intelligences that watch over and assist the struggling aspirants on their upward way. He should daily recall the fact that he is now moving forward toward a freer, richer, more joyous life than he has yet known and that every effort brings him nearer to its realization. Thus dwelling on the subject in its various aspects he creates the ardent desire that serves to propel him forward.

If he feels that these things make an ideal a little too high for him at present he may reach that point by degrees. He may at first dwell in thought upon the personal satisfaction that would come from the possession of astral sight. Let him reflect upon what it would mean to be conscious of the invisible world; to have all its wonders laid open before him; to be able to consciously meet the so-called dead, including his own friends and relatives; to be able to have the positive personal proof that we survive the death of the physical body; to be able to become one of the "invisible helpers" of the world; to have available the priceless advantages of the astral region and to bring the consciousness of all this into the physical life. That is certainly something worth all the time and effort required to attain it.

Thus thinking constantly of the widened life and added powers it would confer, the desire to move forward in self-development will be greatly stimulated. But the student should always keep it in mind that the real purpose of acquiring new powers is to increase his capacity for service to the race, and that he who falls short of that ideal walks upon dangerous ground.

The second requisite is a firm will. It should not be forgotten that an unusual and difficult thing is being attempted in which a person of weak will cannot possibly hope to succeed. Even in the ordinary life of the world considerable will power is essential to success. To succeed in business, to become expert in a profession, or to completely master an art, requires strong will, determination, perseverance.

The difficulties in occult development are still greater and, while it is true that any degree of effort is well worth while, the weaklings will not go far. Only those with the indomitable will that knows neither surrender nor compromise may hope for a large measure of success. Once the will is thoroughly aroused and brought into action every hindrance in the way will be swept aside.

"The human will, that force unseen,
The offspring of a deathless soul,
Can hew a way to any goal
Tho' walls of granite intervene.

* * * * *

"Be not impatient of delay,
But wait as one who understands.
When spirit rises and commands
The gods are ready to obey."

Mighty, indeed, is this force when aroused. But a person may be easily deceived about his will. He is likely to think that his will is much stronger than it really is. He may say to himself, "Oh, yes, I would go through anything for the sake of the higher life and spiritual illumination." But that is no guarantee that after a few months of monotonous work he may not abandon it unless he adopts the wise plan of strengthening his will as he moves forward.

Let him begin this by testing his present strength of will, but let him not be discouraged by the result. He should remember that whatever he lacks in will power he can evolve by proper effort.

To find out whether he really has much strength of will a person may begin to observe to what extent he permits his daily plans to be modified, or entirely changed, by the things that run counter to his will. Does he hold steadfastly to his purpose or does he weakly surrender to small obstacles? Has he the will power to even begin the day as he has planned it? The evening before he decides that he will rise at six o'clock the next morning. He knows there are certain excellent reasons why he should do so and he retires with the matter fully decided. It is positively settled that at exactly six o'clock the day's program shall begin. But when the clock strikes that hour the next morning he feels strongly disinclined to obey the summons.

It involves some bodily discomfort to rise at that moment and he concludes that, after all, perhaps he was a bit hasty the evening before in fixing upon that hour! Whereupon he reconsiders the matter and makes it seven; and when that time arrives he generously extends it to eight o'clock.

The hour, of course, is unimportant. But whatever may have been the hour that was previously determined upon the keeping of that determination is of the greatest importance and the failure to put the resolution into effect is evidence of the possession of a weak will.

Now all this proves that such persons have very little real will power, for they permit the desire for trifling bodily comfort to set their plans aside. Such persons are still slaves to the physical body and weakly permit it to upset carefully outlined programs. They are not yet ready for good work in occult development, where real success can come only to those who have steadfast strength of purpose.

People who fail to assert the will and bring the body into complete subjection probably little realize what a price they pay for a trifling physical pleasure; for until we voluntarily take the right course we have not escaped the evolutionary necessity of compulsion and may reasonably expect sooner or later to be thrown into an environment that will apply the stimulus we still need to arouse the will. It may be unpleasant while it is occurring, but what better fortune could befall an indolent man than to find himself in circumstances where his poverty or other necessity compels him to subordinate bodily comfort to the reign of the will?

Nature provides the lessons we require. We may wisely co-operate with her and thus escape the sting. But so long as we need the lesson we may be quite sure that it awaits us.

All the business activities of the world are developing the will. Through them will and desire work together in evolving latent powers.

Desire arouses will power. A man desires wealth and the desire plunges him into business activities and stimulates the will by which he overcomes all the difficulties that lie in his way. Ardent desire for an education arouses the will of the student and the awakened will triumphs over poverty and all other barriers between him and the coveted diploma.

If a man stands at a lower point in evolution where he has not the ambition for intellectual culture nor for fame nor for wealth, but only the desire for shelter and food, still that primitive desire forces him into action; and while his will power will be evolved only in proportion to the strength of the desire that prompts him, it must nevertheless grow. Instead of rising at a certain hour because the will decrees it he may rise only because he knows his livelihood depends upon it. But he is learning the same lesson—the overcoming of the inertia of the physical body—albeit it is compulsory instead of voluntary. But all this is unconscious evolution. It is the long, slow, painful process. It is the only way possible for those who are not wise enough to co-operate with nature in her evolutionary work and thus rise above the necessity of compulsion.

How, then, may we develop the will when it is so weak that we are still the slaves of nature instead of the masters of destiny? Will power, like any other faculty, may be cultivated and made strong. To do this one may plan in advance what he will do under certain circumstances and then carry out the program without evasion or hesitation when the time arrives. His forethought will enable him to do this if he does not undertake things too difficult at first.

Let him resolve to do at a certain hour some small thing which, in the ordinary course of his duties, he sees is necessary but unpleasant; and then firmly resolve in advance that exactly at the appointed time he will do it. Thus fortified before the trial comes he will probably go successfully through with it. After once deciding upon the time there should be no postponement and not an instant's delay when the moment arrives.

One of the things we have to learn is to overcome the inertia of the physical body and many people are not really awake on the physical plane because they have not done so. To a certain extent they are "dead" within the physical body for it is a condition much nearer death than that supposed death of one who no longer has the physical body. The inert mass of physical matter in which such people are functioning leaves them only half alive until they have aroused themselves from its domination. They remind one of the lines:

> "Life is a mystery, death is a doubt,
>   And some folks are dead
>   While they're walking about!"

This inertia of the physical body that so often renders people nearly useless is very largely a matter of habit and can be overcome to a surprising degree by simply using a little will-power. Everybody is familiar with the fact that it is sometimes much easier to think and act than at other times. But perhaps it is not so well known that the dull periods can invariably be overcome by an effort of the will and the physical body be made to do its proper work.

An actor or lecturer after months of continuous work may find the brain and body growing tired and dull. He may feel when going before his audience that he has not an idea nor the wit to express it were someone else to furnish it. Yet by an effort of the will he can quickly overcome the condition and change from stupidity to mental alertness and intensity of thought.

The self is never tired. It is only the physical body that grows weary. It is true that it has its limitations and must not be overtaxed and driven beyond endurance as a tired horse is sometimes cruelly urged forward with whip and spur. Judgment must always be used in determining one's capacity for work. But that which is to be done should never be done draggingly, with the inertia of the physical body marring the work. We should be fully awake instead of "dead" while we "are walking about." If a person resolves to be the master of the body he may soon acquire the power to arouse it to activity and alertness during all his waking hours, very much as one may acquire the habit of keen observation and be conscious of what is occurring in his vicinity instead of being carelessly unconscious of the major portion of what is going on immediately about him.

This matter of giving attention to the things that may properly engage the mind, and of using the will to arouse and control it, is of very great importance. Is it not what we call "paying attention" that makes the connection between the ego and the objective world? Giving attention is a process of consciousness.

The person who fails in attention misses the purpose of life and throws away valuable time and opportunity. To give attention is to be alive and awake and in a condition to make the most of limited physical life. Yet many people cannot give sustained attention to an ordinary conversation nor direct the mind with sufficient precision to state a simple fact without wandering aimlessly about in the effort, bringing in various incidental matters until the original subject, instead of being made clear, is obscured in a maze of unimportant details or lost sight of altogether.

Such habits of mind should be put resolutely aside by one who would hasten self-development. The attention should be fixed deliberately upon the subject in hand, whatever it may be, and nothing should be permitted to break the connection between that and the mind. Whether it is a conversation or a book, or a manual task, or a problem being silently worked out intellectually, it should have undivided attention until the mind is ready for something else.

Perhaps few of us give to any subject the close attention which alone can prove its own effectiveness and demonstrate the fact that there goes with such steadily sustained attention a subtle power of extended, or accentuated, consciousness. When ten minutes is given to a certain subject and other thoughts are constantly intruding, so that when the ten minutes have passed only five minutes have actually been devoted to the subject, the result is by no means a half of what would have been accomplished had the whole of the ten minutes been given to uninterrupted attention.

The time thus spent in wavering attention is practically without effect. The connection between mind and subject has not been complete. Mind and subject were, so to say, out of focus. Attention must be sustained to the point where it becomes concentration.

The mind must be used as a sun-glass can be used. Hold the glass between sun and paper, out of focus, for an hour and nothing will happen. A yellow circle of light falls on the paper and that is all. But bring it into perfect focus, concentrating the rays to the finest possible point, and the paper turns brown and finally bursts into the fire that will consume it. They are the same rays that were previously ineffective. Concentration produced results.

The mind must be brought under such complete control of the will that it can be manipulated like a search-light, turned in this direction or that, or flung full upon some obscure subject and held steadily there till it illuminates every detail of it, as the search-light sends a dazzling ray through space and shows every rock and tree on a hillside far away through the darkness of the night.

The third necessity is keen intelligence. The force of desire, directed by the will, must be supplemented by an alert mind. There is a popular notion that good motives are sufficient in themselves and that when one has the desire to attain spiritual illumination, plus the will to achieve, nothing more is needed but purity of purpose. But this is a misconception.

It is true that the mystic makes devotion the vital thing in his spiritual growth; and it is also true that the three paths of action, knowledge and devotion blend and become one at a higher stage. But while there are methods of development in which intellect is not at first made a chief factor it can by no means be ignored in the long-run; nor are we now considering those methods. A good intellect, therefore, is a necessary part of the equipment.

Good motives play a most important part, indeed, in occult progress. They safeguard the aspirant on his upward way. Without pure motives, without a large measure of unselfishness, the greatest dangers would encompass him. But good motives cannot take the place of good sense and relieve him of the necessity of thinking. He must develop judgment and discrimination. There are things he must know, and he must use his knowledge, or difficulties will follow no matter how noble may be his intentions. Suppose, for illustration, that two men set out upon a dark might to cross a wild and rugged piece of ground—one with bad motives and the other with good. One is going out to rob a house and if need be, to kill anybody who might try to interfere with his plans.

His motives are very bad but he has perfect knowledge of the dangerous ground he is to cross and he will therefore travel over it in safety. The other man has the best of motives. He is going to spend the night with a sick and helpless neighbor. But he has no knowledge of the rough and treacherous ground he must cross in the darkness and his good motives will not insure him against stumbling over the stones or falling into a ditch and breaking his arm. Good motives are not enough. We must know! Progress in occultism is impossible without knowledge.

But how is a keen, alert intelligence to be acquired if we do not possess it? Like any other latent faculty or power it may be evolved. As the physical strength may be steadily increased by constant exercise of the muscles, so mind may increase in power by systematic work. It should be exercised in original thinking. A stated period, if only a quarter of an hour daily, can be set aside for the purpose.

A book on a serious subject will furnish material but the too common method of reading, of following the author lazily and accepting whatever he sets forth as a matter of course, is of little value. One must read with discrimination, receiving the ideas offered as a juryman would receive testimony from a witness, considering it from every possible viewpoint, examining it in the light of known facts, turning it over in the mind, weighing it thoughtfully, and accepting or rejecting according to its reasonableness or its lack of reason. In such mental work for intellectual growth each paragraph can be considered by itself and only a small portion of the time should be given to the reading while the remainder is devoted to pondering over what has been read. Of course a specific study is an advantage and perhaps nothing is better than to study occultism, thinking deeply upon the problems of human evolution.

Another method that goes admirably with such work is the close observation and study of all the life in manifestation about us. We should try to comprehend people, to observe and understand them. Every word, act and facial expression has its meaning to be caught and interpreted. All this will not only sharpen the wits but also strengthen human sympathy for it enables us the better to know the difficulties and sorrows of others. If such practices are followed faithfully day by day the growth will be steady.

Still another useful practice is to exercise the imagination, the art of creating mental pictures with no physical object present. The face of an absent friend can be called up in the mind and reproduced in every detail—the color of the eyes and hair, the various moods and expressions. Or one's childhood home can be recalled and the imagination made to reconstruct it. The house being complete the landscape can be reproduced, with the hills, trees and roads. Repeated practice at "seeing mentally" is of the greatest value in occult development.

While the aspirant is thus working to improve the three essential qualifications of desire, will and intelligence—to intensify his desire to possess powers for the helping of others, to strengthen the will to get such powers, and to steadily improve the intellect—he should also be giving most earnest attention to meditation, for it is through this practice that the most remarkable results may be produced in the transformation of his bodies, visible and invisible, through which the ego manifests itself in the physical world.

In the degree that these are organized and made sensitive and responsive they cease to be limitations of consciousness. Such sensitiveness and responsiveness may be brought about by meditation, together with proper attention to the purification of the physical and astral bodies; for purity and sensitiveness go together.

Meditation is a subject so very important to the aspirant that specific instructions should guide him. The average person, used to the turbulent life of occidental civilization, will find it a sufficiently difficult matter to control the mind, and to finally acquire the power to direct it as he desires, even with all the conditions in his favor.

The serene hours of morning are the most favorable of the twenty-four for meditation. Regularity has a magic of its own and the hour should be the same each morning. To be alone in surroundings as quiet as possible is another essential. The most desirable time for meditation is soon after awakening in the morning. Before turning the mind to any of the business affairs of the day let the aspirant sit calmly down and mediate upon any wholesome thought, like patience, courage or compassion, keeping the mind steadily upon the subject for five minutes.

Two very important things are being accomplished by such meditation. First, we are getting control of the mind and learning to direct it where and how we choose; and, second, we are attracting and building into the bodies we possess certain grades of imponderable matter that will make thinking and acting along these lines easier and easier for us until they are established habits and we actually become in daily life patient, courageous and compassionate. Whatever qualities or virtues we desire to possess may be gained through the art of meditation and the effort to live up to the ideal dwelt upon daily by the mind.

While it is absolutely true that any human being can make of himself that which he desires to be—can literally raise himself to any ideal he is capable of conceiving—it must not be supposed that it can be done in a short time and by intermittent effort.

We sometimes hear it said that all we need do is to realize that all power is within us, when, presto! we are the thing we would be! It is quite true that we must realize their existence before we can call the latent powers into expression; but the work of arousing the latent into the active is a process of growth, of actual evolutionary change.

The physical body as it is now is not sensitive enough to respond to subtle vibrations. Its brain is not capable of receiving and registering the delicate vibrations sent outward by the ego, and the task of changing it so that it can do so is not a trifling or easy one. But every effort produces its effect and to the persistent and patient devotee of self-development the final result is certain. But it is not a matter of miraculous accomplishment. It is a process of inner growth.

There are, it is quite true, cases in which people who have entered upon this method of self-development have, in a short time, attained spiritual illumination, becoming fully conscious of the invisible world and its inhabitants while awake in the physical body; extending the horizon of consciousness to include both worlds, and coming into possession of the higher clairvoyance that enables one to trace past causes and modify impending effects. But such people are those who have given so much attention to self-development in past lives that they have now but little more to do in order to come into full possession of occult powers.

Sometimes it requires little more than the turning of their attention to the matter. Becoming a member of the Theosophical Society or seriously taking up theosophical studies is sometimes the final step that leads to the opening of the inner sight.

But how can one know to what point he may have advanced in the past and where he now stands? How may we know whether there is but a little work ahead or a great deal? We cannot know; nor is it important to know. The person who should take up the task merely because he thinks there is little to do would certainly fail.

The very fact that he would not venture upon the undertaking if he thought the task a difficult one is evidence that he has not the qualifications necessary for the success of the occult student. Unless he is filled with a longing to possess greater power to be used in the service of humanity, and fired with an enthusiasm that would hesitate at no difficulties, he has not yet reached the point in his evolution where he awaits only the final steps that will make him a disciple.

But even the absence of the keen desire for spiritual progress, which is the best evidence of the probability of success, should not deter anybody from entering upon the systematic study of theosophy and devoting to it all the time and energy he can; nor should the thought that many years might pass without producing any very remarkable results lead him to conclude that the undertaking would not be a profitable one. The time will come with each human being when he will step out of the great throng that drifts with the tide and enter upon the course of conscious evolution, assisting nature instead of ignoring her beneficent plan; and since it is but a question of time the sooner a beginning is made the better, for the sooner will suffering cease.

There should be a word of warning about the folly of trying to reach spiritual illumination by artificial methods. Astral sight is sometimes quickly developed by crystal gazing and also by a certain regulation of the breathing. For two reasons such methods should be avoided. One is that any powers thus gained can not be permanent, and the other is that they may be more or less dangerous. Many people have made physical wrecks of themselves or have become insane by some of these methods.

There are those who advertise to quickly teach clairvoyance, for a consideration, as though spiritual powers could really be conferred instead of evolved! It is true that efforts toward the evolution of such powers may be enormously aided by teachers, but such instruction can not be bought, and the offer to furnish it for money is the best evidence of its worthlessness.

Those who teach this ancient wisdom select their own pupils from the morally fit, and tuition can be paid only in devotion to truth and service to humanity. That is the only road that leads to instruction worth having, and until the aspirant is firmly upon that sound moral ground he is much better off without powers, the selfish use of which would lead to certain disaster.

But how shall the pupil find the teacher? He need not find him, at first, so far as the limited consciousness is concerned. Long before he knows anything of it in his waking hours he may be receiving instruction while he is out of the physical body during the hours of sleep. The teacher finds the pupil long before the pupil suspects that the teacher exists; and since it is the pupil who has the limited consciousness it is quite natural that it should be so.

Thus it is inevitable that all who enter upon the way that leads to spiritual illumination must long remain ignorant of the fact that any teachers are interested in them or that anybody is giving the slightest attention to them. Naturally enough one cannot know until the moment arrives when his brain has become sufficiently sensitive to retain a memory of at least a fragment of his superphysical experiences.

But what leads to the selection of the pupil? His earnestness, his unselfishness, his devotion, his spiritual aspirations. There is an old occult maxim to the effect that when the pupil is ready the Master is waiting. They have need of many more than are ready to be taught. Those who lead and enlighten watch eagerly for all who will qualify themselves to enter upon the upward way.

Every human being gets exactly what he fits himself to receive. He cannot possibly be overlooked. By his spiritual aspiration each lights the lamp in the window of his soul and to the watchers from the heights that light against the background of the overwhelming materiality of our times must be as the sun in a cloudless sky.

Other things come later but these simpler things, to realize the necessity for conscious evolution, to comprehend the method of soul development, to take full control of the mind and the physical body, to resolutely curb the grosser desires and to give free rein to the higher aspirations are the first infant steps in the self-development that leads to illumination. Then we begin to discover that this very desire for greater spiritual power is generating a force that carries us forward and upward. We soon begin to observe actual progress.

The brain becomes clearer, the intellect keener. Our sphere of influence grows wider, our friendships become warmer. Aspiration lifts us into a new and radiant life, and the wondrous powers of the soul begin to become a conscious possession. And to this soul growth there is no limit.

The aspirant will go on and on in this life and others with an ever-extending horizon of consciousness until he has the mental grasp of a Plato, the vivid imagination of a Dante, the intuitive perception of a Shakespeare.

It is not by the outward acquirement of facts that such men become wise and great. It is by developing the soul from within until it illuminates the brain with that flood of light called genius.

And when, through the strife and storm, we finally reach the tranquility of the inner peace we shall comprehend the great fact that life really is joy when lived in the possession of spiritual power and in perfect harmony with the laws of the universe. With even these first steps in occult achievement the aspirant enters upon a higher and more satisfactory life than he has ever known.

Literally he becomes a new man. Gradually the old desires and impulses fade away and new and nobler aspirations take their place. He has learned obedience to law only to find that obedience was the road to conquest.

He has risen above the gross and sensuous by the power of conscious evolution; and, looking back upon what he has been with neither regret nor apology, he comprehends that significant thought of Tennyson: On stepping stones of their dead selves men rise to higher things.

THE END

9 789388 841412